MOTORMANiA

TRUCKS

Written by

PENNY WORMS

W

FRANKLIN WATTS

LONDON•SYDNEY

First published in 2010 by
Franklin Watts
338 Euston Road
London NW1 3BH

Franklin Watts Australia
Level 17/207 Kent Street
Sydney NSW 2000

Series editor: Jeremy Smith
Design: Graham Rich
Cover design: Graham Rich
Picture research: Penny Worms

A CIP catalogue record for this book is available
from the British Library.

ISBN 978 0 7496 9489 0

Dewey classification: 629.2'24

Printed in China

Franklin Watts is a division of Hachette Children's Books,
an Hachette UK company.
www.hachette.co.uk

The author would like to thank Felix Wills and the following
for their kind help and permission to use images: the
communications team at Mack Trucks, Inc. Warren Noakes
for his picture and information about the Centipede, Julian
Dyer at Terex and Benjamin Syring at Daimler AG.

Picture Credits
Joe Baraban/Transtock/Corbis: 19. www.bigfoot4x4.
com: 25c. Steve Collender /Shutterstock: 23c. Ian
Dagnall/Alamy: 24, 29. Daimler AG:8cl, 8tr, 8-9, 14-15,
14cl, 15cr. Paul Drabot/Shutterstock: 27. Sagi Elemer/
Shutterstock: 11. Risteski Goce/Shutterstock: 7tr. Illusion
Studio/Shutterstock: 21bl. JLP/Shutterstock: 5, 26cr. Joyfull/
Shutterstock: 6cl. Lester Lefkowitz/Getty Images: 18c,
18b. Luis Louro/Shutterstock: 26bl. Mack Trucks Inc./12,
13bl, 13cr. MACK is a registered trademark of Mack
Trucks, Inc. All rights reserved. Warren Noakes: 4, 17c. Olly/
Shutterstock: 6-7. Doug Pearson/JAI/Corbis: 16-17. Ryasick
Photography/Shutterstock: 3, 22. Chris Sattlberger/
Getty Images: 16cl, 28. Michael Shake/Shutterstock: front
cover. Maksim Shmeljov/Shutterstock: 25b. Chris Cooper-
Smith/Alamy: 20. Dwight Smith/Shutterstock: 23b.
www.unicat.net: 10t, 10b. Tim Woodcock/Alamy: 21cr.

Disclaimer: Some of the 'Stats and Facts' are
approximations. Others are correct at time
of writing, but will probably change.

CONTENTS

TRUCKS

Trucks (lorries) are the biggest vehicles on our roads. They lift, haul and travel long distances, carrying goods and equipment. Without trucks, many of the things we buy every day would not be there.

TO THE RESCUE

Trucks have many uses, but probably the most important is saving lives. Some trucks are turned into ambulances (left). Some are used for fighting fires. Others carry people and equipment to where they are desperately needed.

POWER TRAIN

All trucks need powerful engines (right). They mostly run on diesel, and the size is dependent on the size of the truck and the loads it has to pull. Trucks need more gears than cars and have more wheels to spread the weight of their loads.

TYPES OF TRUCK

There are two types of truck. A **rigid truck** has a fixed frame. The back and front cannot be separated. An **articulated truck** is in two or more parts (as below). Articulated trucks are known as tractor-trailers, semi-trailers or semi-trucks. The tractor is the cab and engine. This pulls a trailer that can be detached.

UNIMOG

When it comes to trucks, the Mercedes-Benz Unimog is a 60-year-old classic. It is like a mechanical ox – strong, steady and indestructible. It has **all-wheel drive** so it has a great many uses, including tackling wild fires, road building and overland **expeditions**.

HISTORY

The Unimog first appeared after World War II (1939–45). It started life as a farm vehicle. It was more **versatile** than a tractor because it could drive just as well *on* the road as off it. By the 1950s it was popular with armies around the world. Since then, Mercedes have improved it even more.

inflated tyre narrower track *flat tyre wider track*

TYRE TRACTION

The tyres of an off-road truck are as important as its engine. The tyres need good grip, even in thick mud or snow. The Unimog has a system that allows the driver to deflate the tyres at the push of a button. Flatter wheels mean better grip or **traction**.

STATS AND FACTS

- **Vehicle:** Mercedes-Benz Unimog
- **Type:** Off-road truck
- **Country of origin:** Germany
- **Cost:** £80,000 to £130,000
- **Claim to fame:** A 60-year-old classic off-road truck that can go where other trucks can't.

SUPREME OFF-ROADER

The big brother of the Unimog family is the U5000. This supreme off-roader tackles deep snow, flooded roads and cross-country trails, taking people and equipment to wherever they need to go.

UNICAT

Unicat vehicles are for adventurers, explorers and globetrotters. Each Unicat is a cross between a tank, a camper van and a hotel! They are **custom-made** and designed to take you anywhere you want to go in the world – in style.

LUXURY LIVING

In your Unicat, you can have a bathroom, a kitchen, a computer area, a washing machine and luxury beds. You can even have a rack or platform at the back to take a mini car or motorbike along with you. Water, electricity, heating, lights and storage are standard.

PICK A TRUCK

Unicat build their trucks using a Volvo (right), MAN or Unimog (p8-9) truck **chassis**. You can choose which one you would like. Your choice would depend on how much you want to pay, the engine size you need and how much serious off-roading you want to do.

STATS AND FACTS

- **Vehicle:** Unicat
- **Type:** Custom-built off-road truck
- **Country of origin:** Germany
- **Cost:** from £187,000 (new body on pre-owned truck)
- **Claim to fame:** One of the most luxurious heavy goods vehicles in the world.

GO ANYWHERE

Unicats can cross deserts, drive through streams and climb up mountains. Everything you need is onboard. They are ideal vehicles for wildlife camera crews, overland **safaris**, emergency recovery and rallying.

TITAN BY MACK

The Titan by Mack is an American 'big rig', an expert in heavy hauling. It has classic styling with lots of shiny **chrome**, an air horn and a massive front grille. It combines good looks with power, and is an impressive sight thundering down US or Australian highways.

Cab

Front grille

Trailer

MULTI-PURPOSE

The Mack Titan is a semi-truck. The cab is behind the engine, rather than over it as with most European models. The Mack Titan can pull just about any trailer and can be turned into a heavy-haul **dump truck**. The Mack Titan is also a popular choice to pull Australian road trains (p16).

STATS AND FACTS

- **Vehicle:** Mack Titan
- **Type:** Semi-truck or big rig
- **Country of origin:** USA
- **Cost:** from £22,000 to £113,000
- **Claim to fame:** One of the biggest names in trucks in both the US and Australia.

THE MACK BULLDOG

Every Mack truck has a bulldog on its nose. The bulldog became the company's symbol after World War I (1914–18). The story behind the symbol is that British soldiers referred to Mack trucks as being like bulldogs – strong, fighting dogs that never give up.

MACK TITAN

The Mack Titan has the biggest engine ever fitted into a Mack truck. It produces 515 **horsepower**, which in simple terms means the pulling power equal to 515 horses! But for heavy hauling, **torque** is just as important as engine power. Torque is the force produced by the engine that turns the huge wheels.

MERCEDES-BENZ ACTROS

The Actros is a cab-over road truck, which means the driver's cab is over the engine. These types of trucks are popular in Europe, to pull all sorts of trailers. The Actros has many clever features. It can even scan the road ahead to help drivers keep their distance or stay in lane.

HOME AWAY FROM HOME

Long journeys can mean driving for days. The driver has to sleep in the truck, so comfort is important. In the larger Actros, you can have a soft bed, shaving mirror, towel rail and a table for your breakfast.

STATS AND FACTS

- **Vehicle:** Mercedes-Benz Actros 3355S
- **Type:** Trailer-truck
- **Country of origin:** Germany
- **Cost:** £50,000 to £100,000
- **Claim to fame:** The Actros won the International Truck of the Year Award in 2009.

SAVING FUEL

The Actros runs on diesel. It can use only 19.44 litres per 100 km. That might not sound a lot, but for a powerful engine pulling heavy loads, it is one of the most **fuel-efficient** trucks around.

ACTROS FAMILY

The Actros cab comes in different sizes. The smaller cabs are ideal for short hauls. The larger models are for long-distance hauling. The extra height is for the bed.

ROAD TRAIN

The road trains of Australia are the longest trucks in the world. They often have three or four trailers, joined together and pulled by American-style big rigs. They are an awesome sight on the straight, empty roads of the Australian outback.

Kangaroo bars

BEWARE KANGAROOS

The bars at the front of a road train are called kangaroo bars. They protect the truck from any unfortunate impact with kangaroos that have strayed on to the road.

LONG DISTANCE

Australia is a big country. Most of the towns and cities are around the coast. Road trains make it possible for one driver to take a huge load thousands of kilometres, across the **outback**, from coast to coast.

STATS AND FACTS

- **Vehicle:** Road train
- **Type:** Extra-long tractor-trailer
- **Country of origin:** Australia
- **Cost:** over £100,000 depending on its size
- **Claim to fame:** The world record-breaking road train had 79 trailers!

THE CENTIPEDE

The Centipede was one of the longest working road trains. It was 55.32 metres long, had up to six trailers and 110 wheels. An Australian mining company ran two Centipedes to carry metals to a port hundreds of kilometres away. Each truck was so heavy that if the driver took his foot off the **accelerator** at 60 km/h (40 mph), the truck would carry on for 4 km before stopping!

MINING DUMP TRUCK

Earth-hauling dump trucks are the tallest and heaviest trucks in the world. They work in mines, carrying earth and rocks from one place to another. They are so big that the driver has to climb a staircase to get into the cab.

Staircase — Cab — Bed

MASSIVE MOVER

Driving these monsters must be like driving a house, with the cab a tiny room at the front. The cab has to have thick **sound-proofing** because the noise from outside can be deafening!

THE DUMP

Once the **bed** of the truck is full, the driver drives the dump truck to the dump site. Then, with the touch of a button, the bed starts to tip up and the earth and rocks slide out. It takes less than a minute for it to lift completely.

STATS AND FACTS

- **Vehicle:** Liebherr T282B
- **Type:** Earth-hauling dump truck
- **Country of origin:** Germany
- **Cost:** £3.5 million
- **Claim to fame:** The largest earth-hauling dump truck in the world.

THE BIGGEST OF THE LOT

The Liebherr T282B is the biggest dump truck of them all. It can carry up to 365 tonnes of earth and rocks. That is over one and a half times its own weight. Its six wheels are almost 4 metres high.

CRANE TRUCK

Crane trucks are mobile movers. They lift and move heavy loads, and can travel to wherever they are needed. They come in all sizes, but the big **telescopic boom cranes** are the tallest of them all. The boom has tubes that fit inside one another, which extend out like a telescope.

Boom

Driver's cab

Outrigger

Crane operator's cab

STRONG LEGS

All crane trucks have legs called outriggers. They extend out from the truck's body, two on each side. The outriggers drop down until they meet the ground, and then the truck's wheels can be lifted slightly off the ground. This makes the crane stable, secure and balanced.

STATS AND FACTS

- **Vehicle:** Terex Demag AC700
- **Type:** Crane truck
- **Country of origin:** Germany
- **Cost:** £4 million
- **Claim to fame:** It used to be the most powerful telescopic crane but it now has an even bigger brother.

BOOM TIME

The Terex Demag AC700 is a powerful telescopic crane. When the boom is down, it is only 20 metres long. In the air, it can extend to 60 metres. It can go even taller with attachments added!

TWO CABS

Truck cranes have two cabs. The big one at the front is where the driver sits to drive the truck. The other is on the top of the truck. This is where the crane operator sits to work the crane.

FIRE TRUCK

Fire trucks are probably the most amazing trucks on our roads. Some are huge, with big ladders to reach high places. Others are small and fast to carry rescue teams to a fire quickly. The most common is the 'pumper'. This is a cross between a people carrier, a water tank and a huge toolbox.

LADDER TRUCK

Underneath all the ladders, side storage, lights and hoses is a regular truck chassis. Companies turn it into a firefighting machine. It is like a giant jigsaw puzzle, fitting everything together in the neatest and safest way.

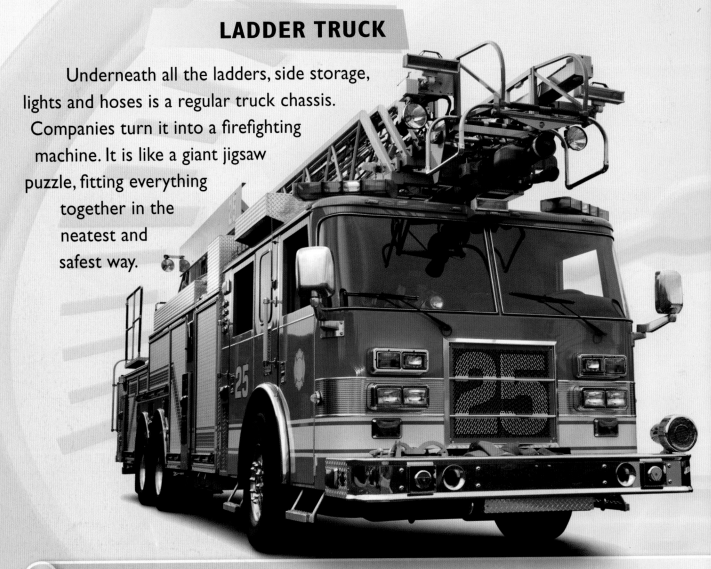

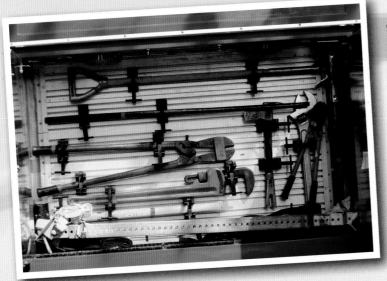

TOOL BOX

If you raise the sides of a fire truck, you'll see that it is crammed with essential tools needed to fight fires and rescue people. The tools include the 'Jaws of Life'. This is like a gigantic can opener that cuts people out of crashed cars.

PUMP PANEL

The pump panel is usually at the back or side of the truck. It is a mind-boggling display of dials and switches. The firefighters turn on the water here, and can change how fast the water flows out. They can also see how much water they have left in the tank.

MONSTER TRUCK

The Bigfoot company were the first to crush cars with a monster truck. This has turned into a popular form of entertainment, especially in the United States. The Bigfoot trucks are famous for racing, crushing cars, long jumps and setting world records. They take a normal truck's body and put it on monster wheels.

BIGFOOT NUMBER 5

Bigfoot number 5 is a giant in the world of monster trucks. It is the world's tallest, widest and heaviest. It is a Ford pick-up that sits high on 3-metre tall tyres. The tyres were originally made for a land-train used in the vast snowy state of Alaska by the US Army in the 1950s.

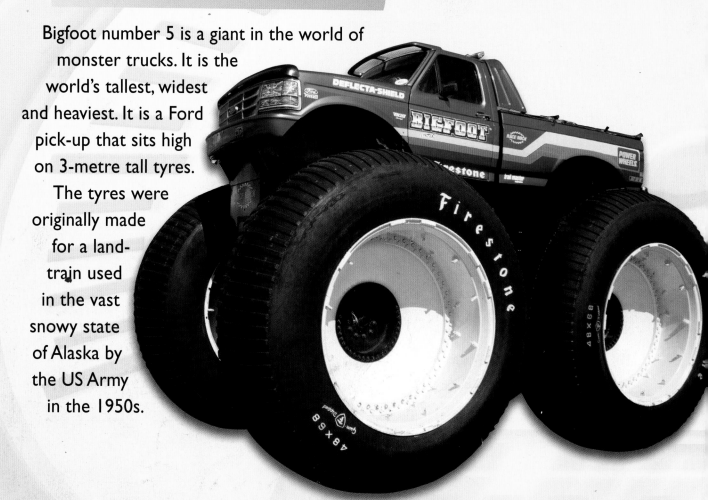

STATS AND FACTS

- **Vehicle:** Bigfoot number 14
- **Type:** Monster truck
- **Country of origin:** USA
- **Cost:** average £100,000 (to build)
- **Claim to fame:** Current world record holder for the monster truck long jump and top speed.

BIGFOOT NUMBER 14

Bigfoot number 14 is not as big as number 5, but it is more talented. It holds the world monster truck long-jump record, jumping over a Boeing 727 plane. At the same time, it also set a monster truck land-speed record of 111.5 km/h (69.3 mph).

INTERNATIONAL MONSTERS

Monster truck shows are now held all over the world. This is Swamp Thing, a UK monster truck competing in the European Championships.

RACING TRUCKS

Truck racing is becoming increasingly popular. The first racing trucks were standard road-going trucks. The drivers would even race them with their trailers! Now, truck racing is an international sport and the trucks are turbo-charged brutes, specially adapted for different races.

TURBO TRUCKS

The engines of racing trucks are far more powerful than road trucks – in a **drag race** they could beat a Porsche 911 over a short distance. They are fitted with **roll cages** and other safety features to protect the driver. Truck racing is supposed to be non-contact, but they crash into one another all the time.

RALLY TRUCKS

Some of the toughest cross-country races, such as the **Dakar Rally**, include a race for trucks. All-terrain trucks, including the Unimog (p8–9) and Unicat (p10–11), are ideal for driving long distances through mountains, forests and across deserts.

STATS AND FACTS

- **Vehicle:** Shockwave
- **Type:** Racing truck
- **Country of origin:** USA
- **Cost:** anywhere from £10,000 to £100,000
- **Claim to fame:** The fastest truck in the world – travelling from 0 to 482 km/h (300 mph) in 11 seconds!

SHOCKWAVE

Shockwave is the fastest truck in the world. It has a top speed of 605 km/h (376 mph). Powered by three jet engines, it needs parachutes to slow it down. Shockwave races planes, not trucks, in special displays in the United States. Fuel is piped directly into burners to create the tail of flames.

GLOSSARY

accelerator the pedal that the driver presses to go faster (also known as the throttle)

all-wheel drive when a vehicle's engine powers all four wheels

articulated truck a truck that has different parts that can be separated from one another, often a tractor and trailer (also known as a semi-truck)

bed (dump truck) the part of the truck that holds all the material that needs to be moved, such as earth and rocks

chassis a chassis is the metal frame that supports a vehicle's body and to which the wheels are attached

chrome short for chromium, a very shiny metal

custom-made when something is adapted to suit the owner's needs or tastes

Dakar Rally the Dakar Rally is a tough, long-distance race that used to run from Paris in France to Dakar in Senegal but has since moved to South America

drag race a type of race in which the vehicles race side-by-side, in a straight line, over a set distance

dump truck a truck with a lifting bed (or bucket) at the back, often used in mines to carry and 'dump' earth, rocks and other material

expedition an organised and adventurous journey, often to somewhere few people go

fuel-efficient burns as little fuel as possible – a fuel-efficient vehicle will use less fuel to travel the same distance as a vehicle that is not fuel-efficient

horsepower the measure of how powerful an engine is – each horsepower is equivalent to the pulling power of one horse

outback a large area of Australia that is hot and dry, and as a result few people live there

rigid truck a truck where all the parts are joined together and cannot be split

roll cage a rigid frame built around the cab of a vehicle to protect the driver from injury if the vehicle rolls over

safaris overland journeys through wild areas, often to see animals and birds in their natural habitat

sound-proofing measures taken to keep out loud noise

telescopic boom cranes cranes with several sections that fit inside one another, and can be extended to reach their full height

torque the force that makes a vehicle move from a standstill

traction how well the vehicle grips a surface – good traction means good grip

versatile something that has lots of uses

INDEX